HŘIMALY

Scale Studies

for Violin

Scale-Studies.

Tonleiter-Studien. —— Etudes de gammes.

C major. Draw a broad tone and change the bow without pausing.
C Dur. *Sehr gezogen, mit breitem Ton; den Bogenwechsel ohne Pausen.*
Ut majeur. Bien tiré, avec ampleur de son, changements des coups d'archets sans interruption.

J. HRIMALY.

A Minor. As above.
A moll. *Wie oben.*
La mineur. Comme plus haut.

F major. The piano must be produced in a soft but clear manner.
F Dur. *Das piano muss leise, aber hell klingen.*
Fa majeur. Le piano doît être doux, mais clair.

D minor. Equal Forte throughout. The Tone strong, but not pressed.
D moll. *Gleiches Forte bis zum Schluss. Der Ton stark, aber nicht gedrückt.*
Ré mineur. Son large et soutenu. Le son fort, mais pas écrasé.

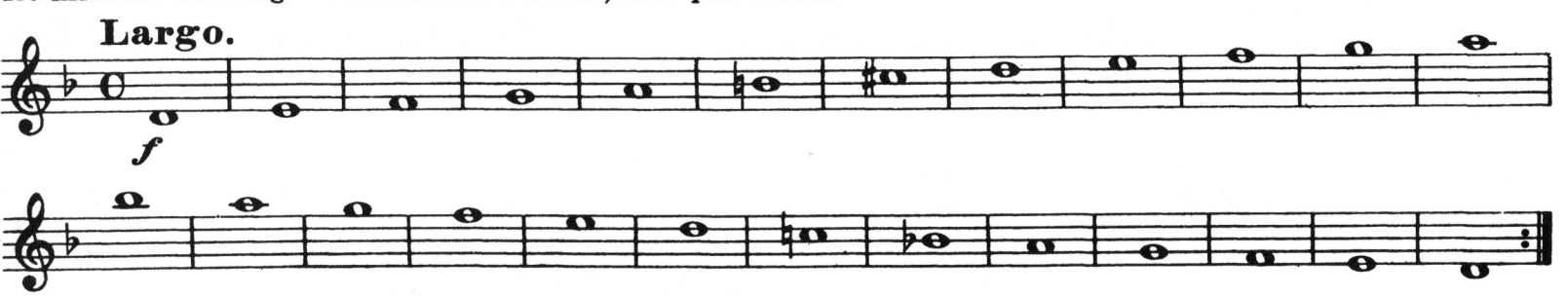

4

Bb Major. Make no pause between the Forte and Piano.
B Dur. *Zwischen dem Forte und Piano keine Pausen machen.*
Si♭ majeur. Pas d'interruptions entre le Forte et le Piano.

G Minor. As above.
G moll. *Wie oben.*
Sol mineur. Comme plus haut.

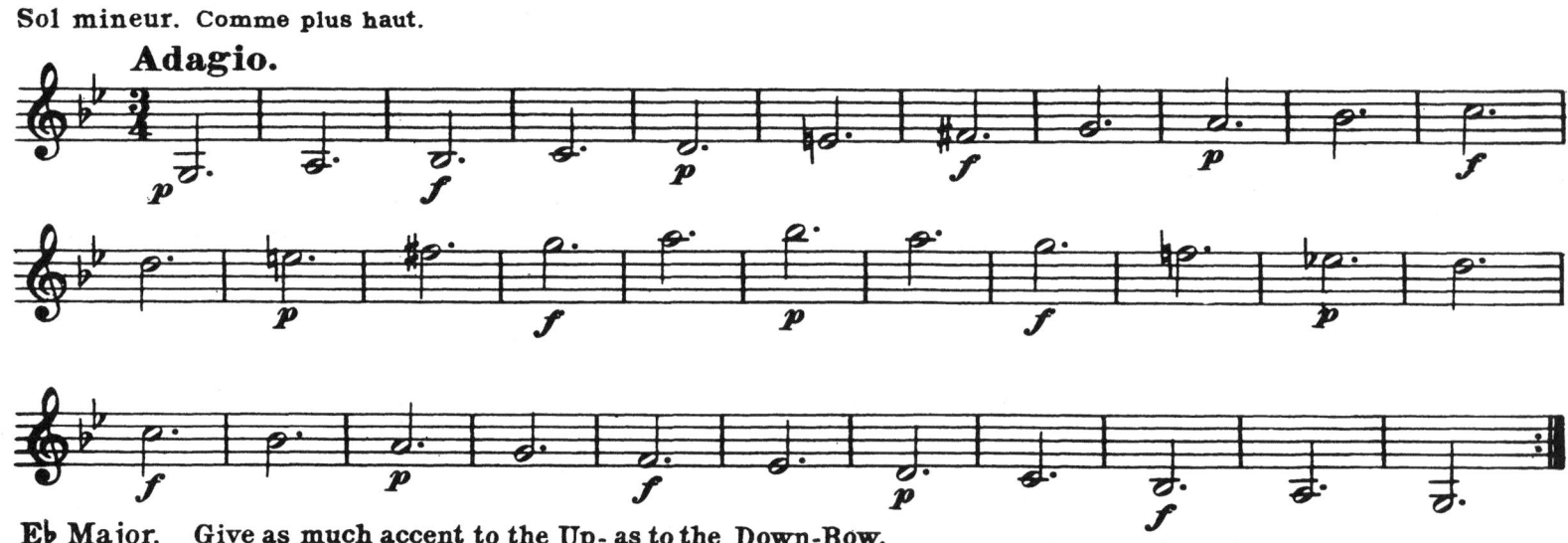

Eb Major. Give as much accent to the Up- as to the Down-Bow.
Es Dur. *Die Accente im Heraufstrich ebenso stark wie im Herunterstrich.*
Mi♭ majeur. Les accents en poussant aussi forts qu'en tirant.

C Minor. As above.
C moll. *Wie oben.*
Ut mineur. Comme plus haut.

Ab Major. (Count two) The quarter note light and short, almost like an eighth.
As Dur. *(2 zählen) Die Viertelnote leicht und kurz, beinahe wie ein Achtel.*
Lab majeur. (Comptez 2) La noire légerè et brève presque comme une croche.

F Minor. As above.
F moll. *Wie oben.*
Fa mineur. Comme plus haut.

Db Major. The quarter note almost like an eighth.
Des Dur. *Die Viertelnote beinahe wie ein Achtel.*
Réb majeur. La noire presque comme une croche.

Bb Minor. As above.
B moll. *Wie oben.*
Sib mineur. Comme plus haut.

Gb Major. Broad and equal tone.
Ges Dur. *Breiten und egalen Ton.*
Solb majeur. Son large et égal.

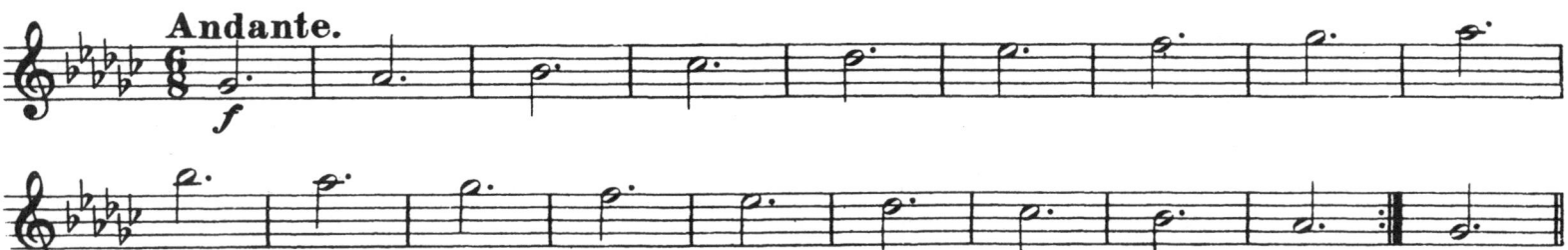

6

E♭ Minor.　As soft as possible, holding the bow very lightly in the hand.
Es moll.　*So leicht wie möglich; den Bogen sehr leicht in der Hand halten.*
Mi♭ mineur. Aussi doucement que possible, tenir l'archet très légèrement dans la main.

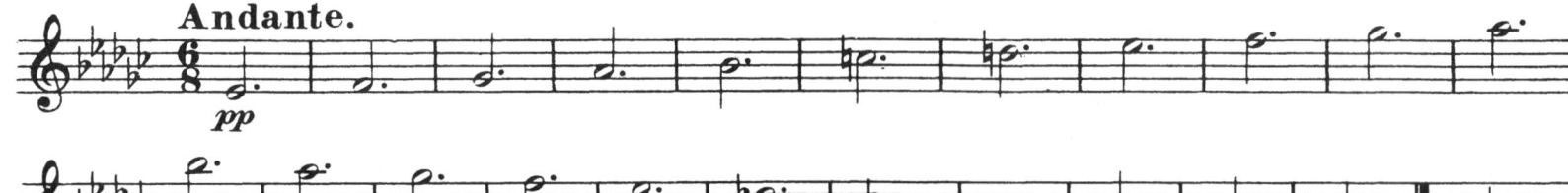

F♯ Major.　With a well marked accent. Make the quarter note short.
Fis Dur.　*Die Viertelnote kurz, den Accent gut markierend.*
Fa♯ majeur. La noire brève, l'accent bien marqué.

D♯ Minor.　As above.
Dis moll.　*Wie oben.*
Ré♯ mineur. Comme plus haut.

B Major.　The quarter must be made somewhat shorter in the same bow.
H Dur.　*Das Viertel in demselben Bogen etwas kürzer abstossen.*
Si majeur. Détachez la noire un peu plus brièvement dans le même coup d'archet.

5908-36

G♯ Minor. The eighth in the same manner as the above quarter.
Gis moll. *Das Achtel wie oben das Viertel.*
Sol♯ mineur. La croche comme plus haut la noire.

Allegretto.

E Major.
E Dur.
Mi majeur.

Allegro agitato.

p poco a poco cresc. f poco a poco dim. p

C♯ Minor.
Cis moll.
Ut♯ mineur.

Allegro agitato.

p poco a poco cresc. f poco a poco dim. p

A Major.
A Dur.
La majeur.

Sostenuto.

mf

F♯ Minor.
Fis moll.
Fa♯ mineur.

Andante moderato.

f

Tempo giusto.

p

Commodo.

p

Moderato.

mf

mf

8

These scales are first to be prac_tised *Legato* and then are to be played with the bowing as given be_low.

The little exercise after each major-scale is intended as a preparatory study to the 6th and 7th steps of the minor scale.

Diese Tonleitern sind erst Legato einzuüben und dann erst mit der unter jeder Tonleiter angegeben_en Strichart zu spielen.

Die Intonation der 6ten und 7ten Stufe in der Molltonleiter wird durch die vorhergehende kleine Fingerübung vorbereitet.

Etudier ces gammes d'abord *legato* et ensuite avec le coup d'archet indiqué sous chaque gamme.

L'intonation des 6me et 7eme degrés dans les tons mineurs sera préparée par l'exercice qui précède les gammes.

B major.
H dur.
Si majeur.

G♯ minor.
Gis moll.
Sol mineur.

E major.
E dur.
Mi majeur.

C♯ minor.
Cis moll.
Ut mineur.

A major.
A dur.
La majeur.

F♯ minor.
Fis moll.
Fa♯ mineur.

D major.
D dur.
Rè majeur.

B minor.
H moll.
Si mineur.

G major.
G dur.
Sol majeur.

E minor.
E moll.
Mi mineur.

For practising major and minor scales within the first position the previous remarks are sufficient.

Dur und Molltonleitern im Umfange der 1ten Position; zum Einüben gilt die Anmerkung der vorhergehenden Nummern.

Tons majeurs et mineurs dans l'étendue de la 1re position; pour les étudier voyez le texte des numéros précédents.

Nº 1.

Major-Scales beginning with the first-finger.

Scales without changing position.

Nº 1.

Dur-Tonleitern mit dem ersten Finger anfangend.

Tonleitern ohne Positionswechsel.

Nº 1.

Gammes dans les tons majeurs à commencer avec le 1er doigt.

Gammes sans changement de position

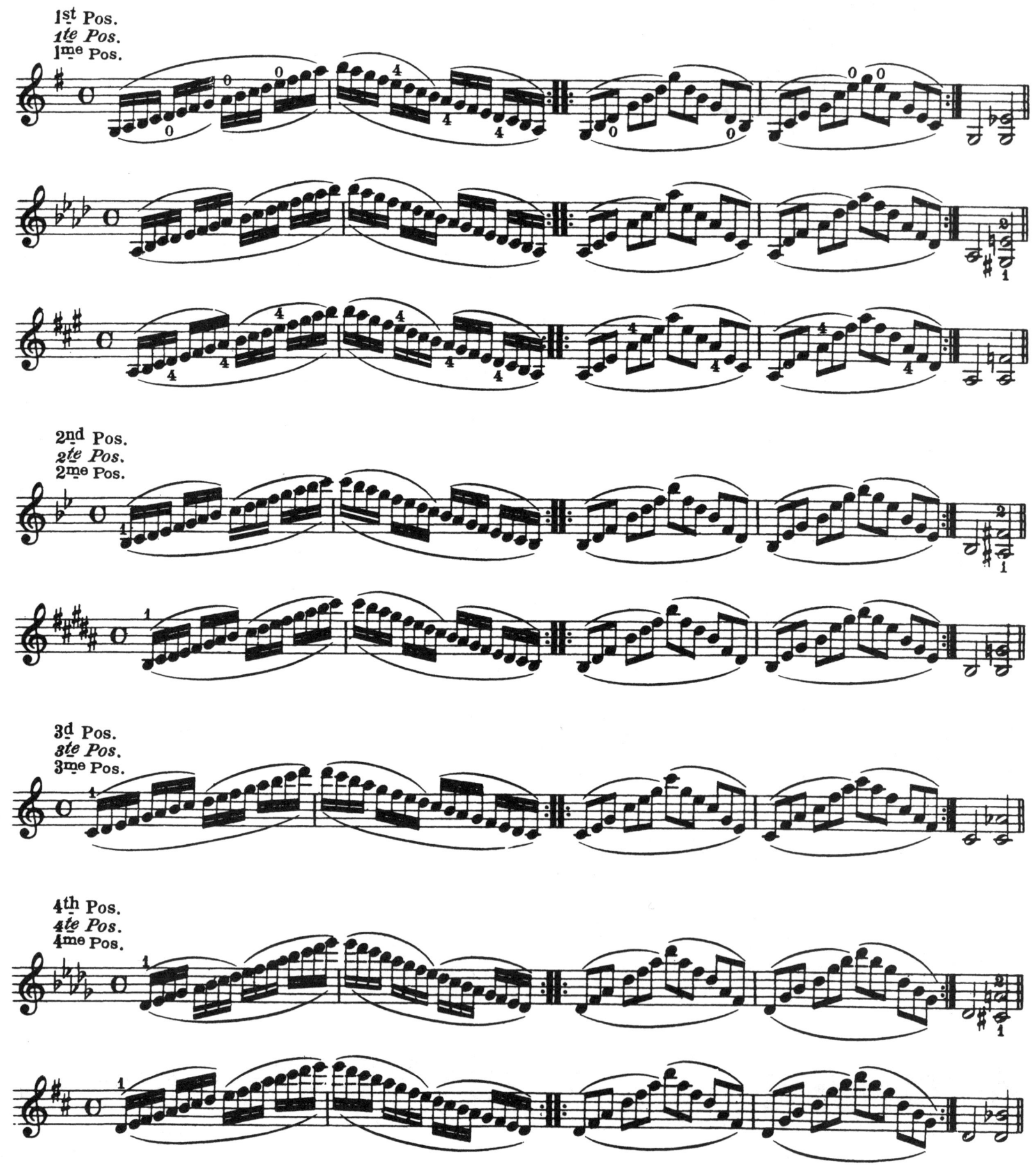

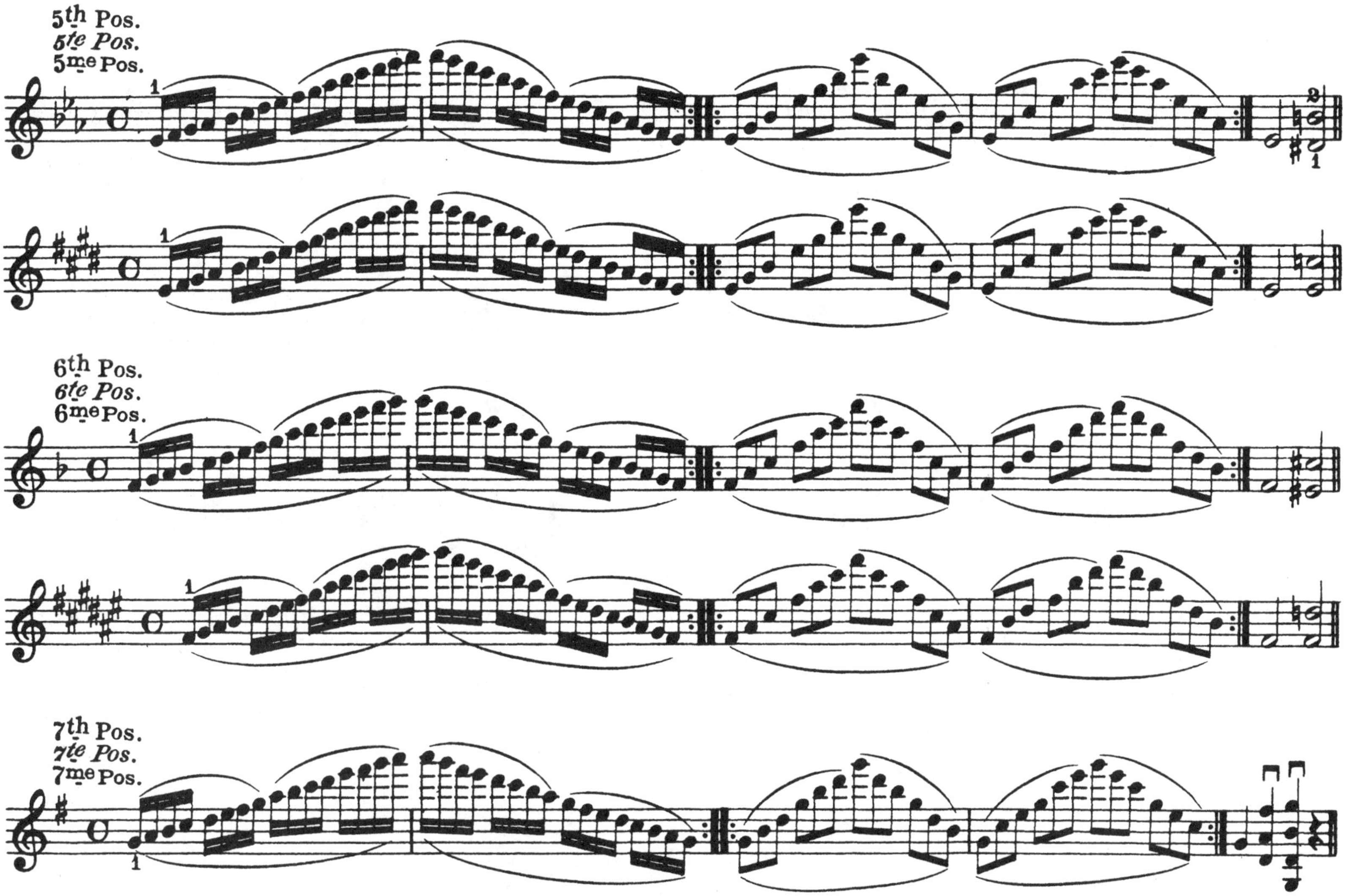

Nº 2.

Minor-Scales beginning with the first finger.

The accents well marked. The first four bowings with the upper half of the bow.

Nº 2.

Moll-Tonleitern mit dem ersten Finger anfangend.

Die Accente gut markieren. Die ersten 4 Stricharten mit der oberen Hälfte des Bogens.

Nº 2.

Gammes dans les tons mineurs à commencer avec le 1er doigt.

Bien marquer les accents. Les 4 premiers coups d'archet avec le haut de l'archet.

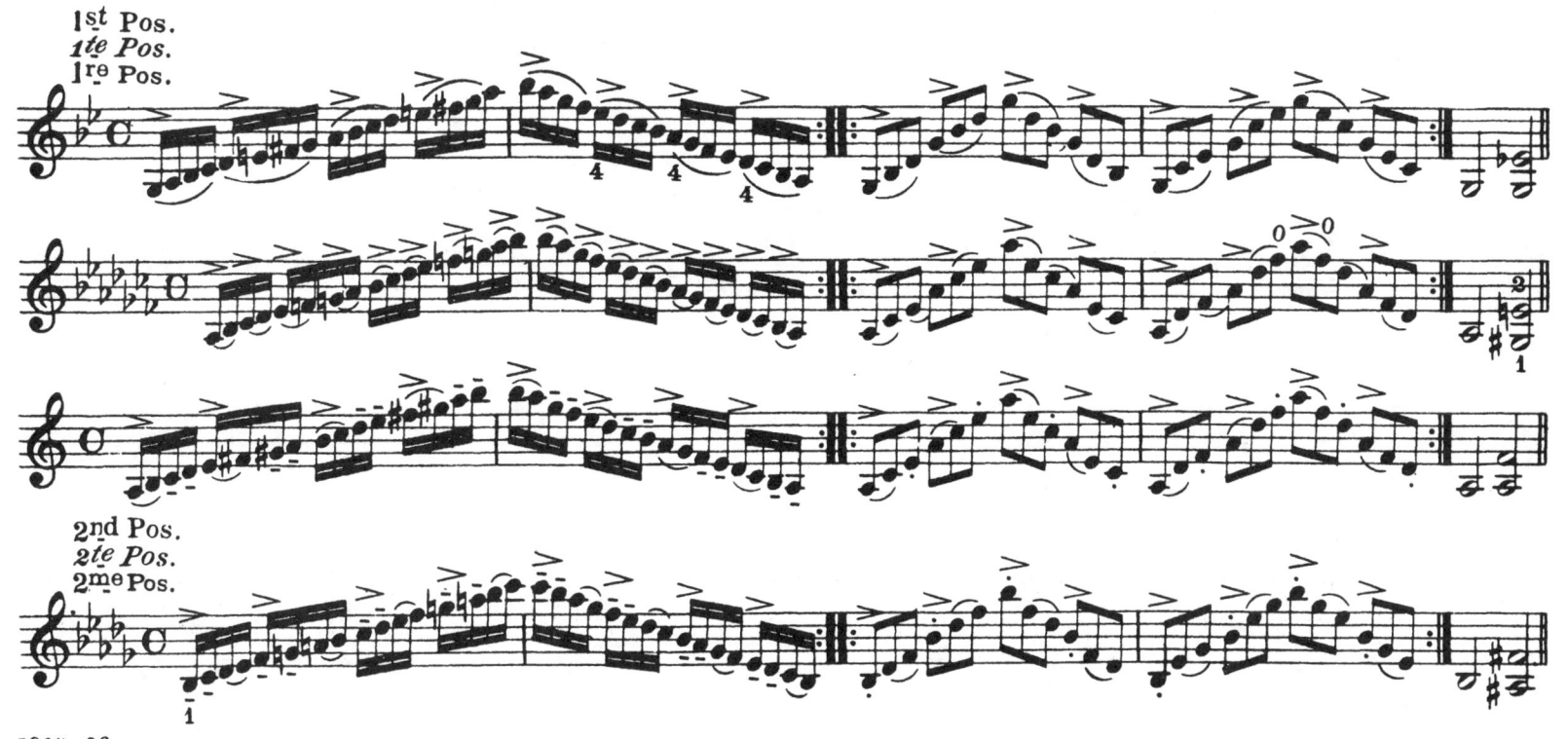

14

On the point and very short and hard. | *An der Spitze sehr kurz und trocken.* | A la pointe, très court et sec.

Martellé.

The first note short and with spirit. | *Die erste Note lebhaft und kurz ao_stossend.* | Détachez la première note vivement et bref.
3d Pos.
3te Pos.
3me Pos.

With half of the bow, a short pause after the third note, and make the last note short. | *Mit halben Bogen, nach der 3ten Note eine kleine Pause; die letzte Note sehr kurz abstossend.* | La moitié de l'archet, faire une petite interruption après la 3me note et détacher la dernière très brièvement.

With bowing of a brisker and livelier character. | *Lebhafter Charakter im Strich.* | Caractère vif dans le coup d'archet.
4th Pos.
4te Pos.
4me Pos.

5th Pos. | *5te Pos.* | 5me Pos.

Nut. Point. Nut. Point. Nut.
Frosch. Spitze. Frosch. Spitze. Frosch.
Talon. à la pointe. Talon. Pointe. Talon.

3/4 of the bow. Softly at the point. 3/4 of the bow. Nut.
3/4 des Bogens. Spitze weich. 3/4 des Bogens. Frosch.
3/4 de l'archet. Pointe doucement. 3/4 de l'archet. Talon.

Accents well marked. Brisk character. | *Accente gut markieren. Lebhafter Charakter:* | Marquer bien les accents. Caractère vif.
6th Pos.
6te Pos.
6me Pos.

Middle. Point.
Mitte. Spitze.
Au milieu. Pointe.

The detached note brisk.
Die gestossene Note lebhaft.
Les notes détachées vives.

7th Pos. | *7te Pos.* | 7me Pos.

5908_36

Nº 3.
Major Scales beginning with the 2nd finger.

Nº 3.
Dur Tonleitern mit dem 2ten Finger anfangend.

Nº 3.
Gammes dans les tons majeurs à commencer avec le 2me doigt.

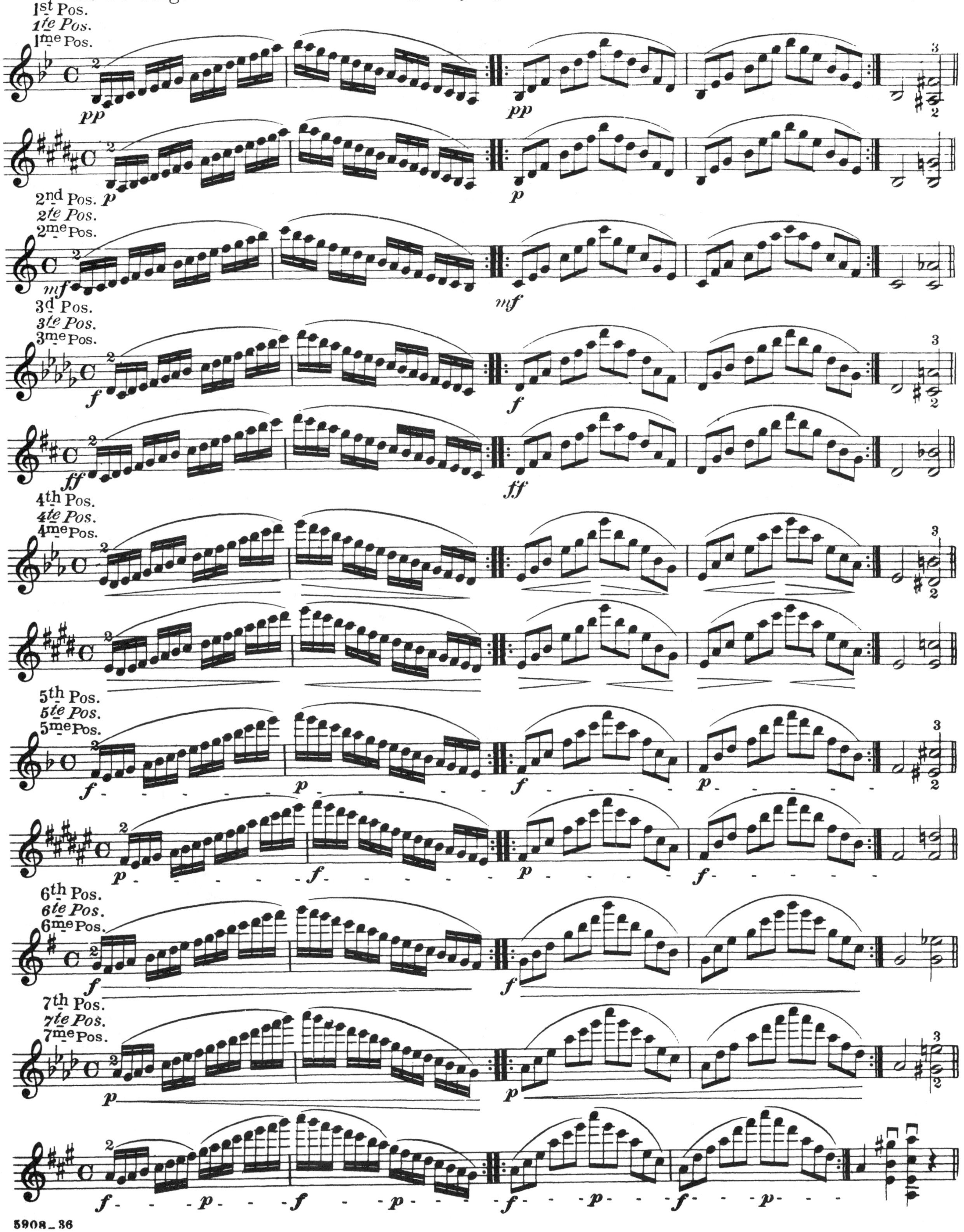

No 4.

Minor Scales beginning with the 2nd finger.

Near the Finger-board and in a soft manner.

No 4.

Moll-Tonleitern mit dem 2ten Finger anfangend.

Weich, am Griffbrett.

No 4.

Gammes dans les tons mineurs à commencer avec le 2me doigt.

Doucement, à la touche.

In the middle of the bow, tolerably quick.

Mitte des Bogens, ziemlich schnelles Tempo.

Au milieu de l'archet mouvement assez animé.

2nd Pos. Middle. Point.
2te Pos. Mitte. Spitze.
2me Pos. Au milieu. A la pointe.

2nd Pos. Point.
2te Pos. Spitze.
2me Pos. Pointe.

Very light Staccato.

Das Staccato sehr leicht.

Le Staccato très léger.

3d Pos. In the middle
3te Pos. In der Mitte
3me Pos. Au milieu

The Rythm must be well marked and all the notes short.

Den Rhythmus gut markieren und alle Noten kurz.

Marquer bien le rhytme et faire toutes les notes courtes (ou brèves.)

4th Pos.
4te Pos.
4me Pos.

Point.
Spitze.
Pointe.

5th Pos. Point.
5te Pos. Spitze.
5me Pos. Pointe.

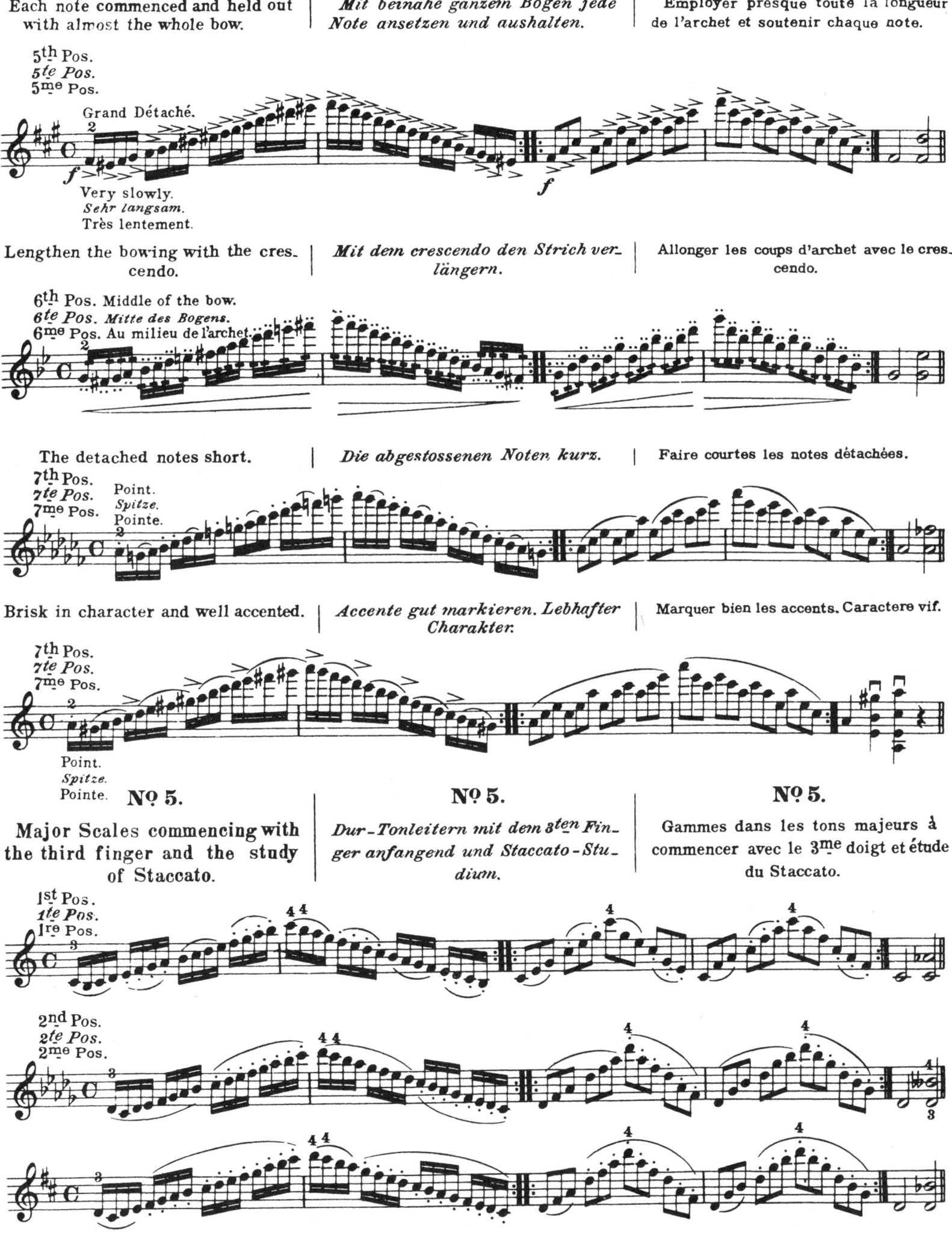

Each note commenced and held out with almost the whole bow.

Mit beinahe ganzem Bogen jede Note ansetzen und aushalten.

Employer presque toute la longueur de l'archet et soutenir chaque note.

5th Pos.
5te Pos.
5me Pos.

Grand Détaché.

Very slowly.
Sehr langsam.
Très lentement.

Lengthen the bowing with the crescendo.

Mit dem crescendo den Strich verlängern.

Allonger les coups d'archet avec le crescendo.

6th Pos. Middle of the bow.
6te Pos. Mitte des Bogens.
6me Pos. Au milieu de l'archet.

The detached notes short.

Die abgestossenen Noten kurz.

Faire courtes les notes détachées.

7th Pos.
7te Pos.
7me Pos.

Point.
Spitze.
Pointe.

Brisk in character and well accented.

Accente gut markieren. Lebhafter Charakter.

Marquer bien les accents. Caractère vif.

7th Pos.
7te Pos.
7me Pos.

Point.
Spitze.
Pointe.

NO 5.

Major Scales commencing with the third finger and the study of Staccato.

NO 5.

Dur-Tonleitern mit dem 3ten Finger anfangend und Staccato-Studium.

NO 5.

Gammes dans les tons majeurs à commencer avec le 3me doigt et étude du Staccato.

1st Pos.
1te Pos.
1re Pos.

2nd Pos.
2te Pos.
2me Pos.

18

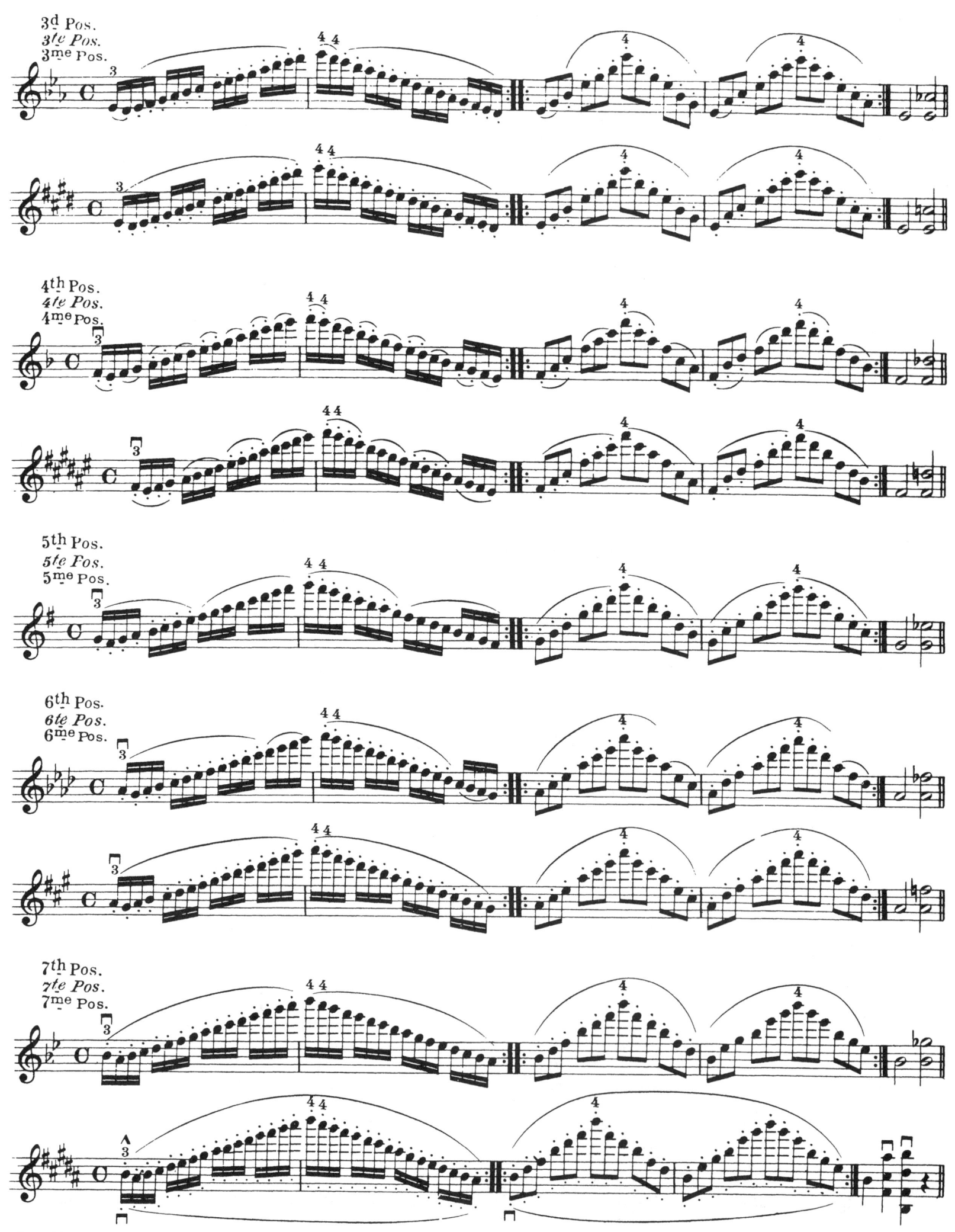

Scales and broken thirds on one string for the development of changing of positions.

The left hand must be held with the greatest ease and the thumb must be very flexible. Exact changing of positions.

Change of the 1st, 3rd and 5th Position.

Tonleitern und Terzengänge auf einer Saite zur Ausbildung des Positionswechsels.

Grosse Leichtigkeit in der Haltung der linken Hand und äusserste Biegsamkeit des Daumens. Präzises Wechseln der Lagen.

Wechsel der 1.3. und 5ten Lage.

Gammes et passages en tierces sur une corde pour former au changement de position.

Grande légèreté dans la tenue de la main gauche et la plus extrême souplesse du ponce. Le Changement de position doit être precis.

Changement de la 1er, 3me, 5me position

Change of the 2nd, 4th and 6th Position. | *Wechsel der 2. 4. und 6ten Lage.* | Changement de la 2me, 4me, 6me position.

Change of the 3d, 5th and 7th Positions. | *Wechsel der 3ten, 5ten und 7ten Lage.* | *Changement de la 3me, 5me, et 7me position.*

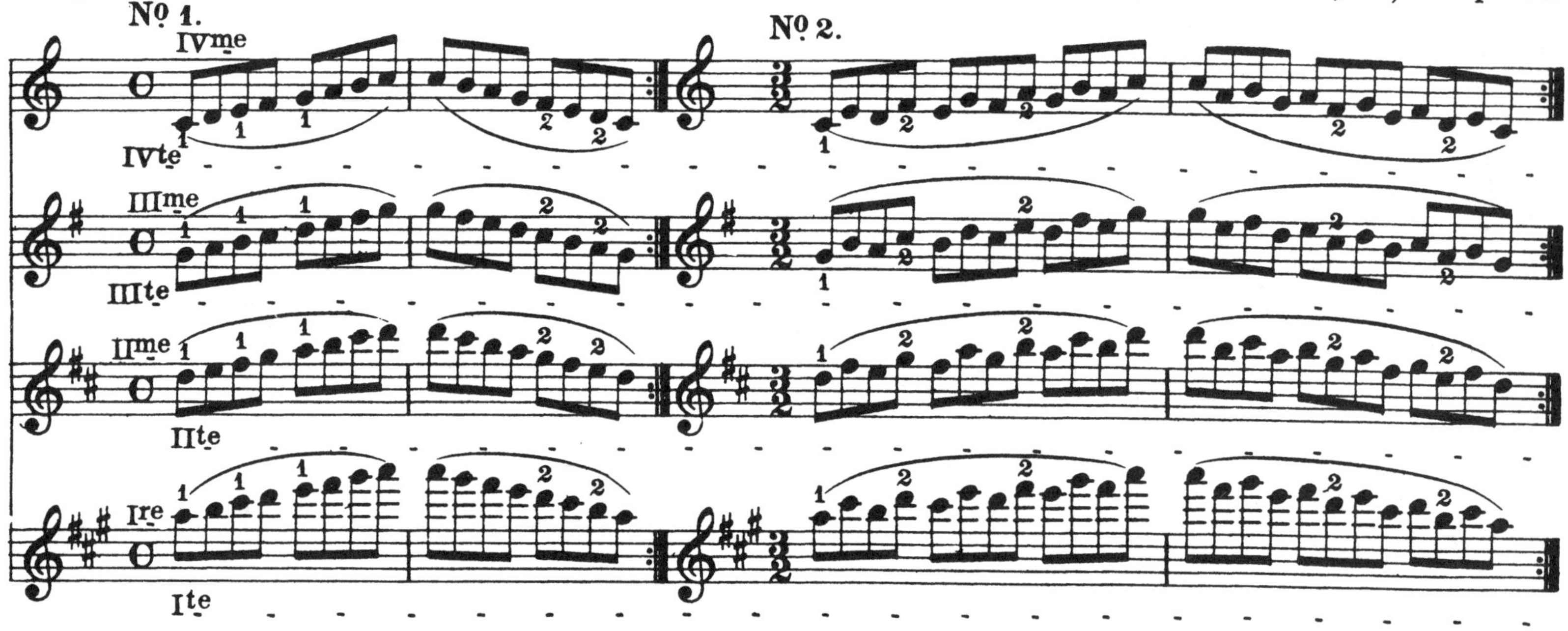

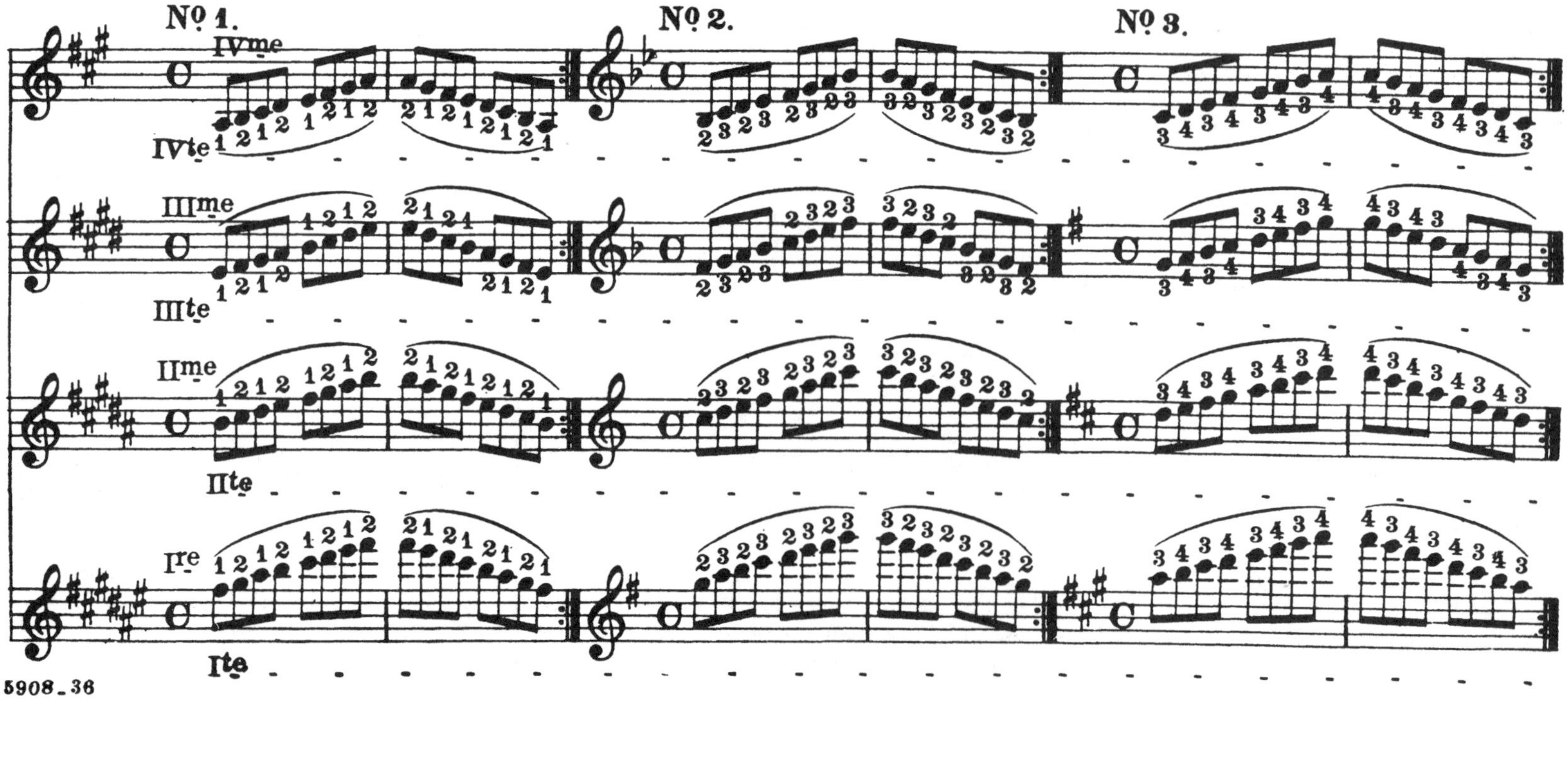

No 7.

Major and Minor Scales and Arpeggios of two octaves, changing positions. *)

No 7.

Zwei-octavige Dur und Moll Tonleitern und Dreiklänge mit Positionswechsel. *)

No 7.

Gammes dans les tons majeurs et mineurs sur 2 octaves et Accords parfaits avec changement de position. *)

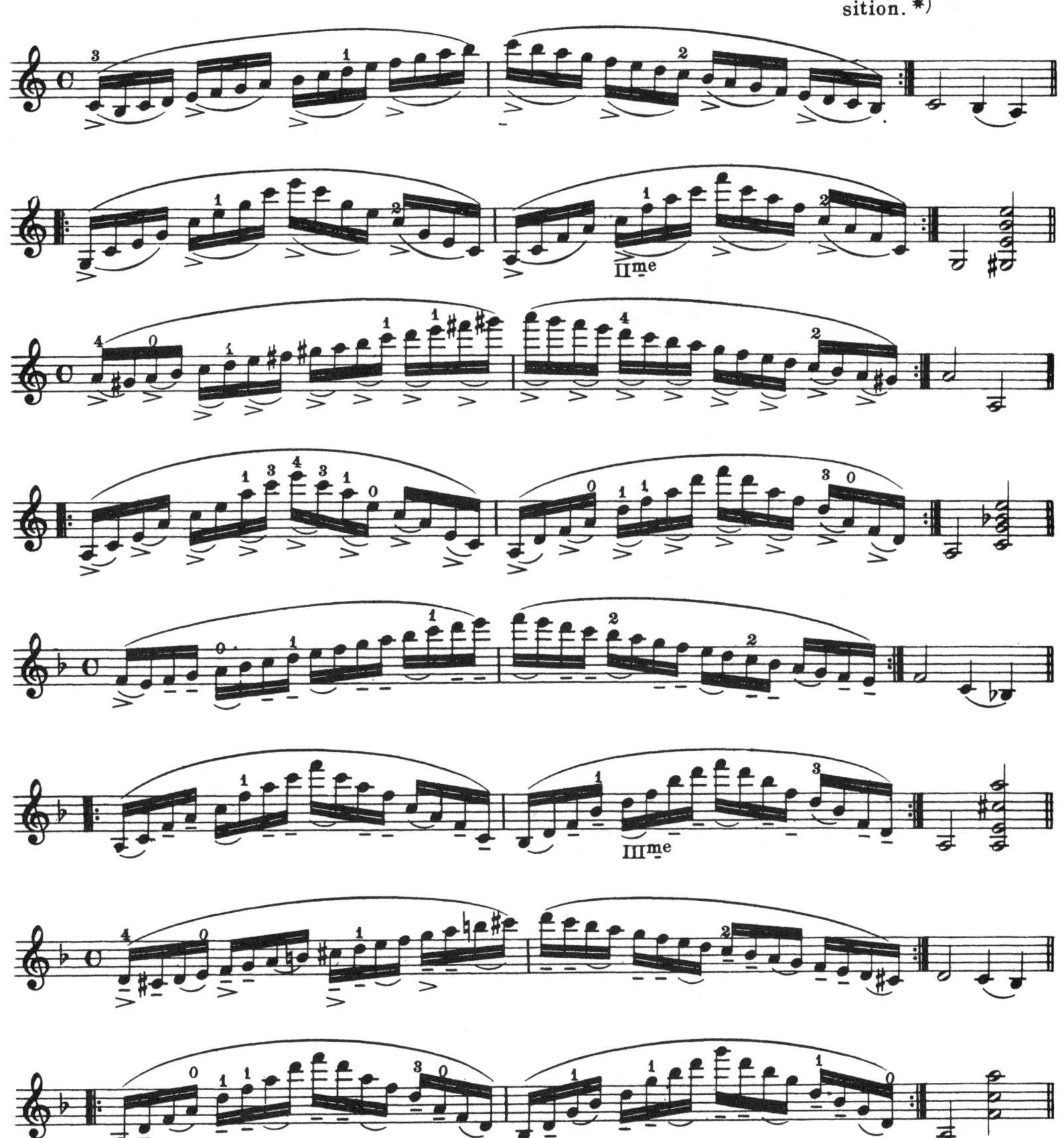

*) Each of these scales must be first practised *legato* and then the bowing and shading as given below, should be practised.

*) *Jede dieser Tonleitern muss erst* legato *geübt werden und erst darnach soll die unter der Tonleiter angegebene Strichart und Nüancirung vorgenommen werden.* *)

*) Etudier ces gammes d'abord *legato*, ensuite avec le coup d'archet et les nuances indiquées sous chacune.

22

detached. *détaché.*

detached. *détaché.*

hammered. *martellé.*

hammered. *martellé.*

5908-36

Springing. *Springbogen*. Sautillé.

Springing. *Springbogen*. Sautillé.

23

5908-36

restez.

IIIme
IIIrd

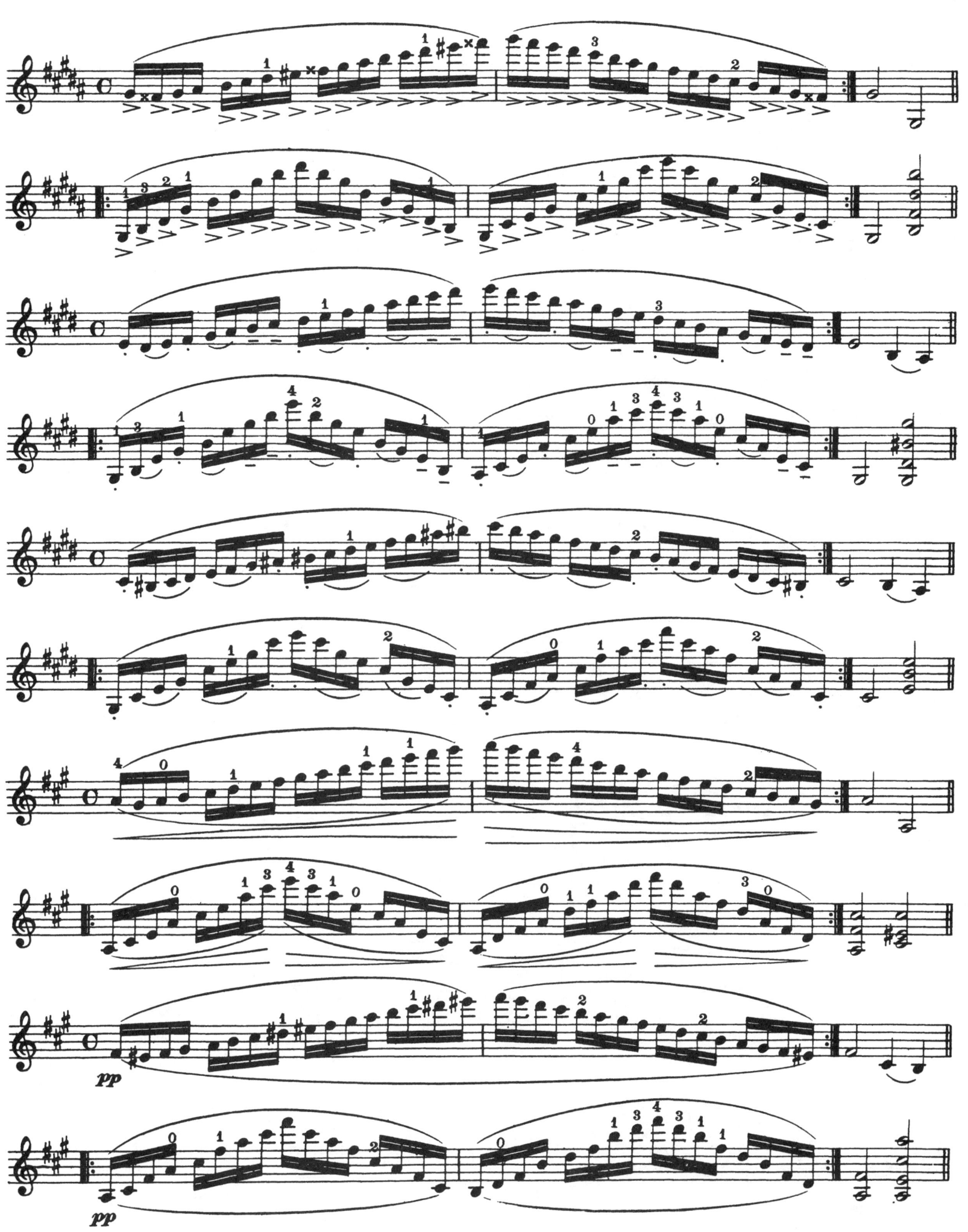

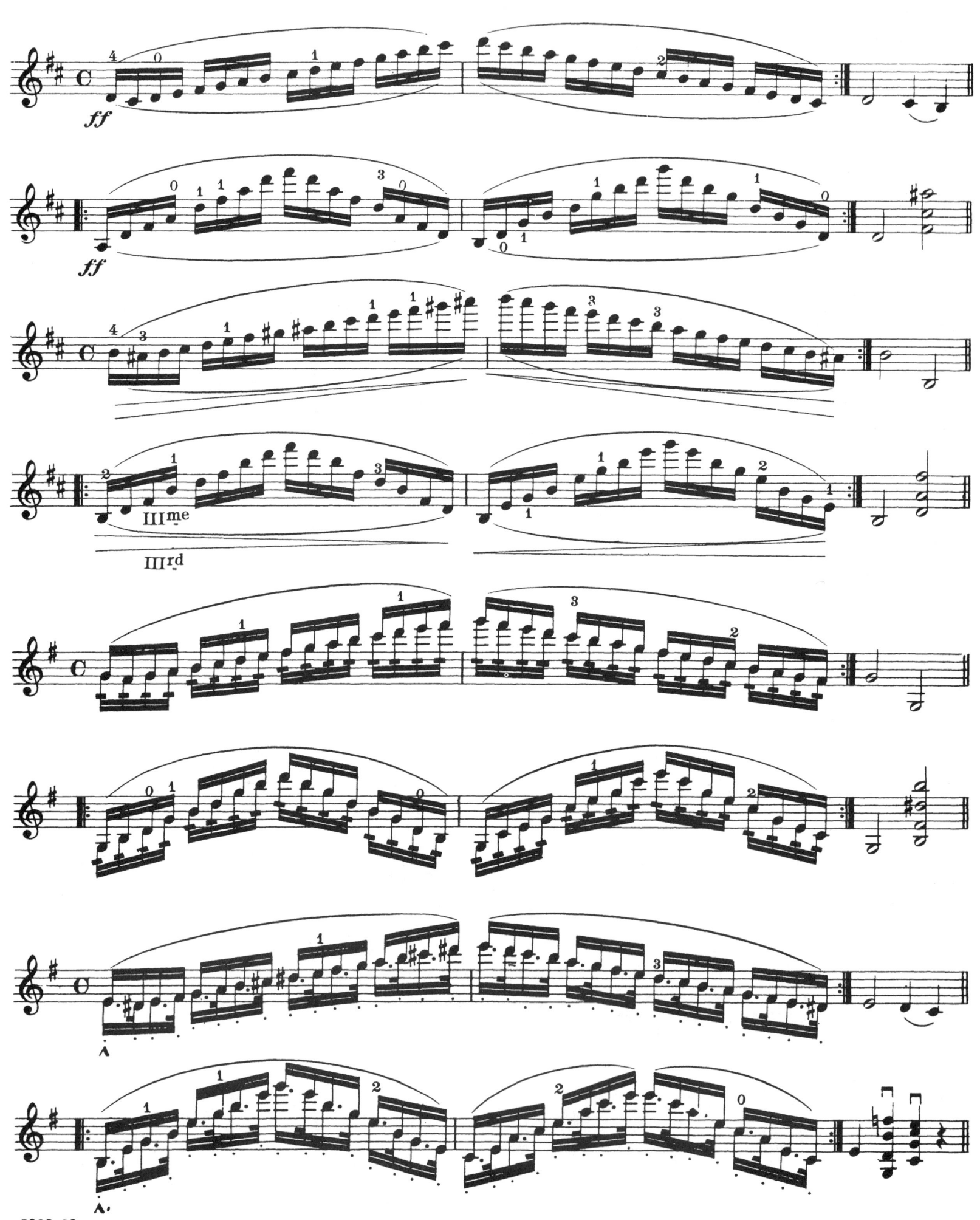

Nº 8.

Extended change of Positions in exercises on one string.

Nº 8.

Erweiterter Positionswechsel durch Uebungen auf einer Saite.

Nº 8.

Extension du changement de position par des exercices sur une corde.

Connection of the 1st with the 3d, 5th and 7th position.

Verbindung der 1ten mit der 3ten, 5ten und 7ten Lage.

Combinaison de la 1re avec la 3me, 5me et 7me position.

Note: These exercises are to be commenced in a slow tempo and to be gradually increased to *Allegro vivace.* Impure intonation and unevenness should be the best hint to teacher and pupil to return to a slower speed.

Anm: *Diese Uebungen sind im langsamen Tempo anzufangen und bis in's* Allegro vivace *(jedoch nach und nach) auszuarbeiten. Unreinheit in der Intonation und Ungleichheit in der Bewegung der Finger der linken Hand sollen für Lehrer und Schüler der beste Wink sein um zu einem langsamen Tempo zurückzukehren.*

Remarque: Commencer ces exercices lentement et les travailler peu a peu jusqu'en *Allegro vivace.* De fausses notes et de l'irregularite dans le mouvement des doigts sont le meilleur indice pour le maitre est pour l'éléve de retourner a un mouvement plus lent.

The following exercises are also to be practiced on the remaining 3 strings in the same manner.

Die folgenden Uebungen sind in der eben angegebenen Weise auch auf den übrigen 3 Saiten zu üben.

Etudier les exercices suivants de la manière, qui vient d'être indiquée aussi sur les 3 autres cordes.

Connection of the 2,4,6,8 position.
Verbindung der 2,4,6,8, Lage.
Combinaison de la 2,4,6,8me position.

Also in *F, C, G major* on the *D, A, E* strings.
Ebenso in F,C,G dur *auf der* D,A,E *Saite.*
De même en *Fa, Ut, Sol majeur* sur les cordes de *Re, La* et *Mi.*

Connection of the 3d, 5th, 7th and 9th positions.
Verbindung der 3ten, 5ten, 7ten und 9ten Lage.
Combinaison de la 3me, 5me, 7me et 9me position.

Also on the *D, A* and *E* strings in *G, D* and *A major.*
Ebenso auf der D, A *und* E *Saite in* G, D, A *dur.*
De même sur les cordes de *Ré, La* et *Mi* en *Sol, Ré* et *La majeur.*

Connection of the 3d, 4th, 5th, 6th, 7th, 8th, 9th and 10th positions.
Verbindung der 3ten, 4ten, 5ten, 6ten, 7ten, 8ten, 9ten, 10ten Lage.
Combinaison de la 3me jusqu'à la 10me position.

Nº 9.

| Changing fingers on one tone.*) | Auswechseln desselben tones durch einen anderen Finger.*) | Remplacement d'un doigt par un autre pour la même note.*) |

These exercises like the previous ones are to be played on all the strings.
Diese Uebungen sind wie die vorigen auf allen 4 Saiten zu üben.
Ces exercices seront exécutés comme les précédents sur les 4 cordes.

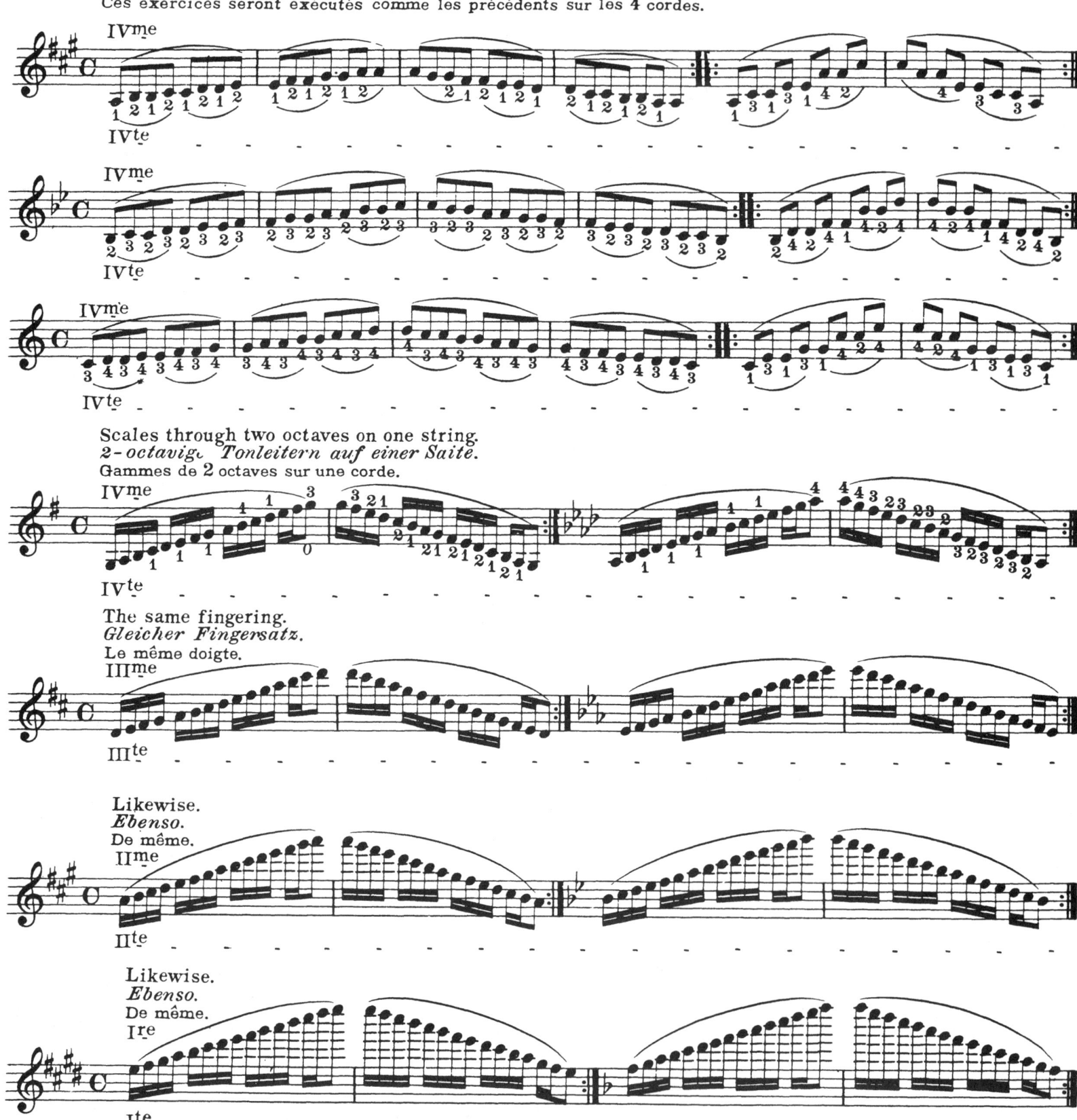

Scales through two octaves on one string.
2-octavige Tonleitern auf einer Saite.
Gammes de 2 octaves sur une corde.

The same fingering.
Gleicher Fingersatz.
Le même doigté.

Likewise.
Ebenso.
De même.

Likewise.
Ebenso.
De même.

*)*Note:* One should not overlook this seemingly unimportant exercise, the great value of which consists in changing fingers on one tone.

*)*Anm:* *Man übergehe ja nicht diese anscheinend unbedeutende Uebung, deren grosser Nutzen eben in dem Auswechseln eines Tones durch einen andern Finger besteht.*

*)*Remarque:* Il ne faut pas negliger cet exercice qui parait peu important, mais dont l'avantage consiste justement dans le remplacement d'un doigt par un autre.

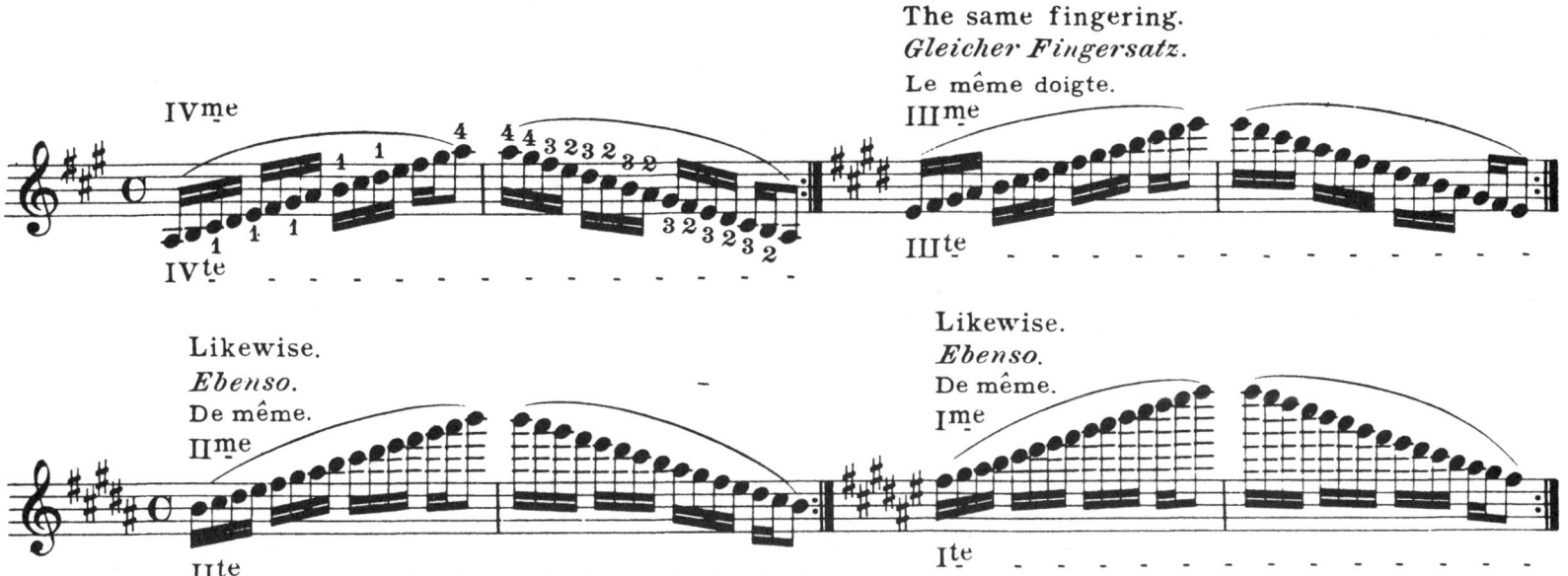

After learning the foregoing, the following 3 octave scales will hardly offer any difficulties to the pupil, but I will not neglect giving him some good advice with regard to them: Usually it is the 3rd octave which presents difficulties; in order to save time, and enable the whole attention to be given to the intonation, it will be well for the pupil to practise the 3rd octave alone in the following manner; the minor scales in particular, with their raised 6th and 7th in ascending and lowered 6th and 7th in descending, are those, which give some pupils much trouble, and to the intonation of which special attention should be paid by the teacher.

The fingerings are, of course, those which are used in the full 3 octave-scales.

Nach dem bisher Gelernten werden dem Schüler die jetzt folgenden 3-octavigen Tonleitern wohl kaum Schwierigkeiten machen, jedoch übergehe er ja nicht den guten Rath, den ich ihm hierbei geben möchte: Gewöhnlich ist es die 3te, das ist die höchste Octave der Tonleiter, welche dem Schüler Schwierigkeiten macht; um Zeit zu sparen und seine Aufmerksamkeit ganz der Intonation zuzuwenden, ist es gut, wenn der Schüler blos die 3te Octave in der hier angegebenen Weise übt; besonders sind es die Moll-Tonleitern, deren im Hinaufgehen erhöhte und im Heruntergehen erniedrigte 6te und 7te Stufe so manchem Schüler viel Mühe macht und auf deren Intonation der Lehrer seine Schüler besonders aufmerksam machen sollte.

Die Fingersätze sind natürlich die, welche bei den vollständigen 3-octavigen Tonleitern hier in Anwendung kommen.

Après avoir appris tout ce qui a été traité jusqu'ici l'élève ne trouvera aucune difficulté à exécuter les gammes suivantes sur 3 octaves, mais qu'il n'oubile pas le bon conseil que nous voudrions lui donner: c'est en général la 3me octave, la plus haute de la gamme qui présente des difficultés pour l'élève; pour gagner du temps et attirer son attention tout spécialement sur la justesse il sera bon qu'il n'étudie que la 3me octave de la manière indiquée. Sachant les gammes dans les tons mineurs avec le 6me et 7me intervalle qui sont haussées d'un ½ ton en montant et baissées en descendant créent des difficultés pour l'élève et le maître devrait attirer l'attention de l'élève spécialement sur la justesse de ses gammes

Les doigtés sont naturellement ceux qui sont appliqués en exécutant les gammes dans l'étendue de 3 octaves.

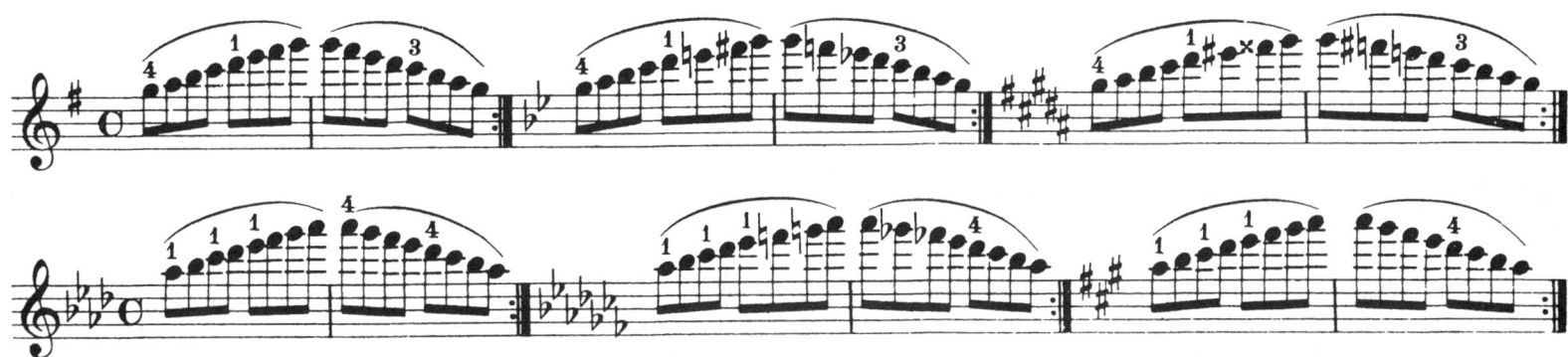

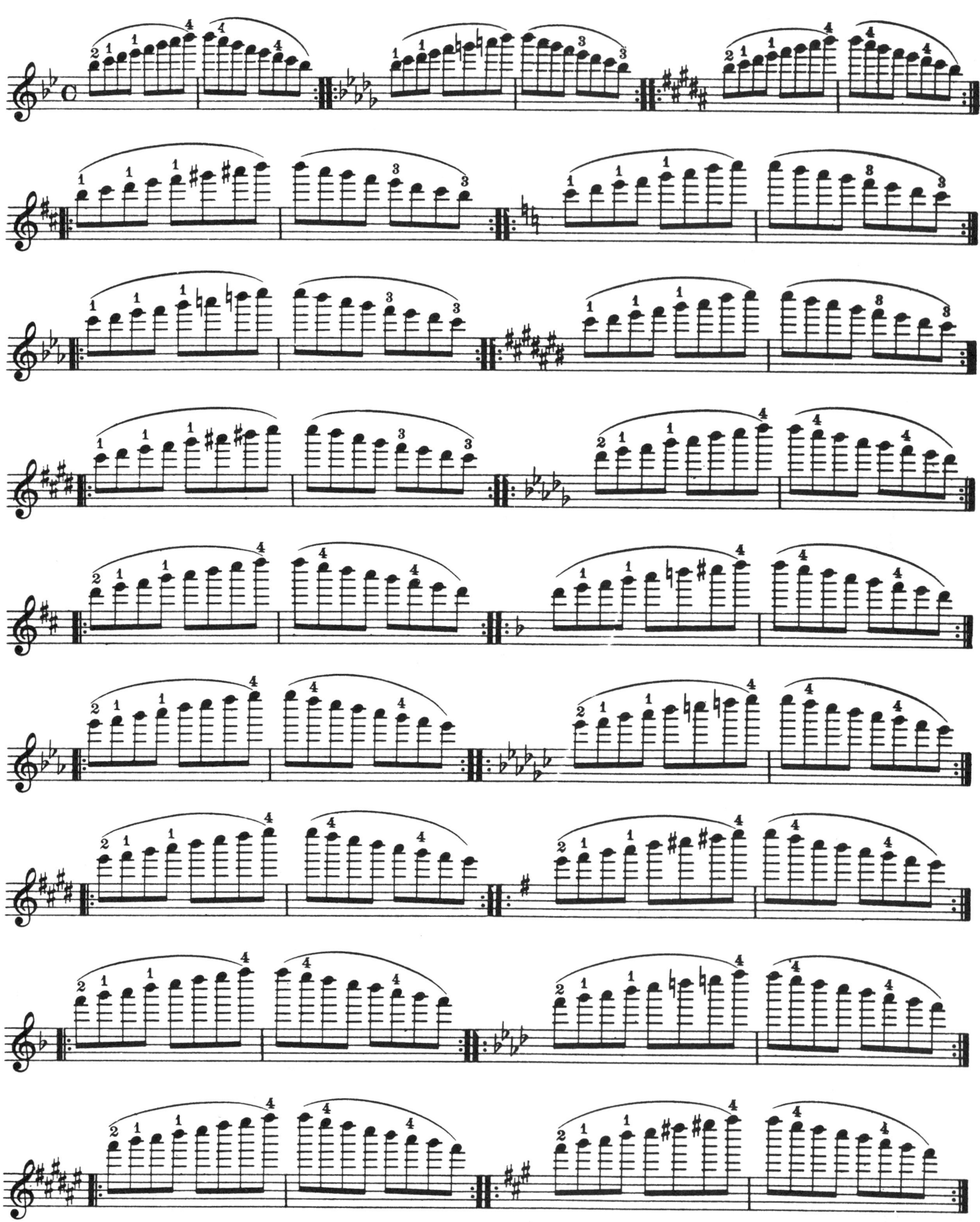

№ 10.

The scales through three octaves are to be played in every tempo from *Andante* to *Vivace* and with every kind of bowing. The bowings are to be taken from Nos. 2, 4 and 5.

№ 10.

Die dreioctavigen Tonleitern sind in jeden Tempo vom Andante *bis zum* Vivace *und mit allen möglichen Stricharten zu spielen. Die Stricharten sind aus № 2, 4 und 5 zu nehmen.*

№ 10.

Les gammes sur 3 octaves doivent s'exécuter dans chaque mouvement, de l'*Andante* jusqu'au *Vivace* et de tous les coups d'archet possibles. Pour ces manières diverses voyez les sections 2, 4 et 5.

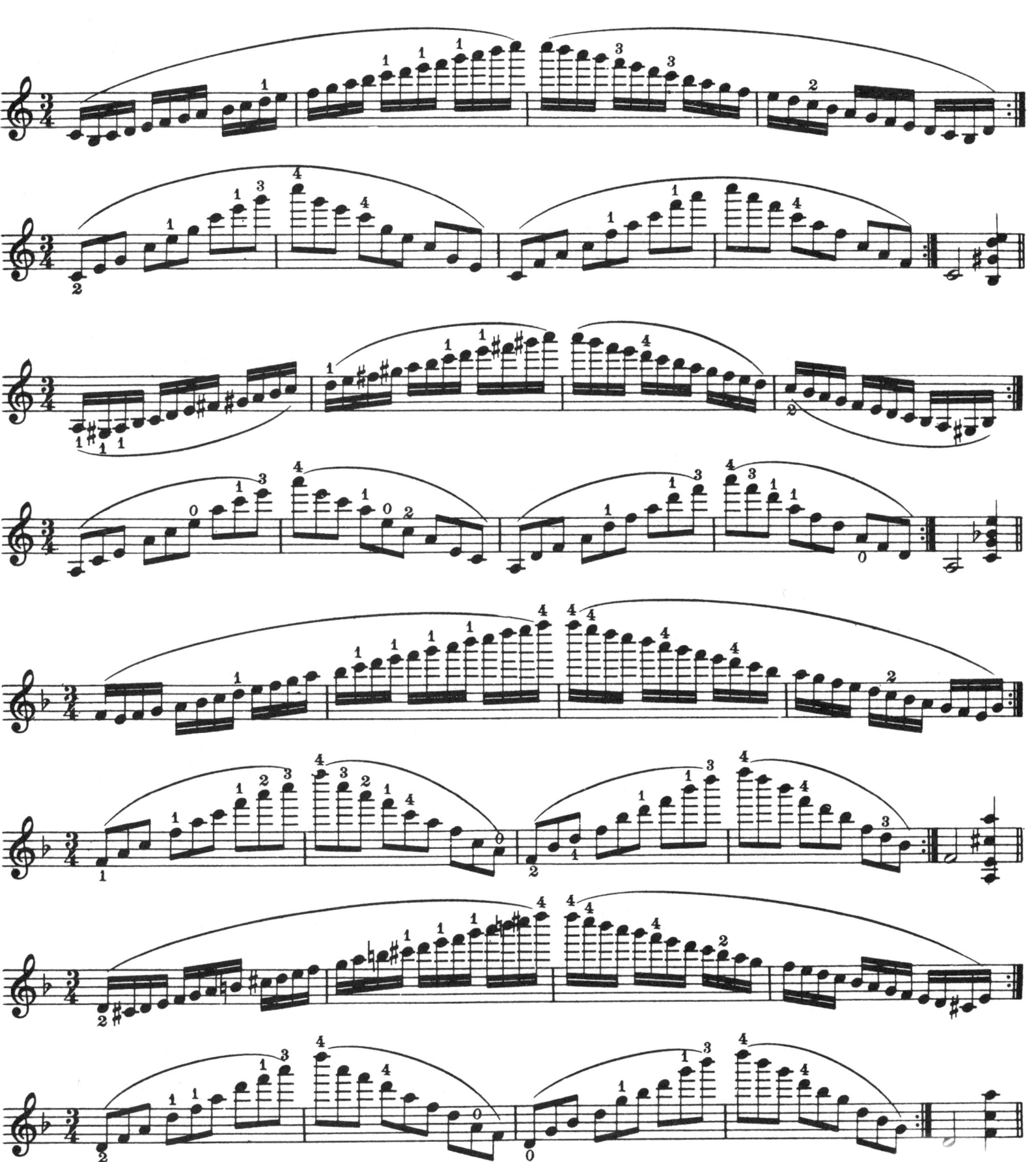

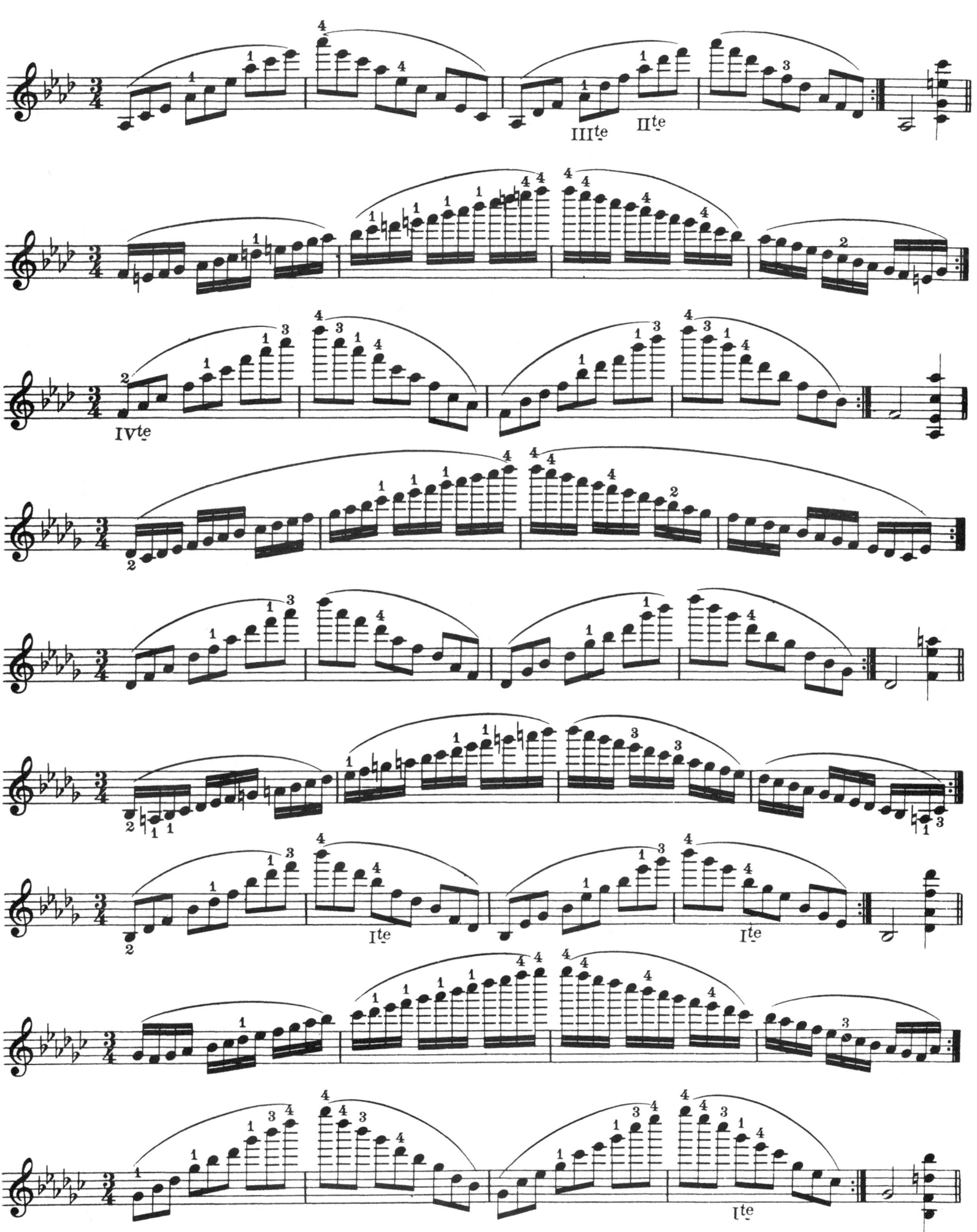

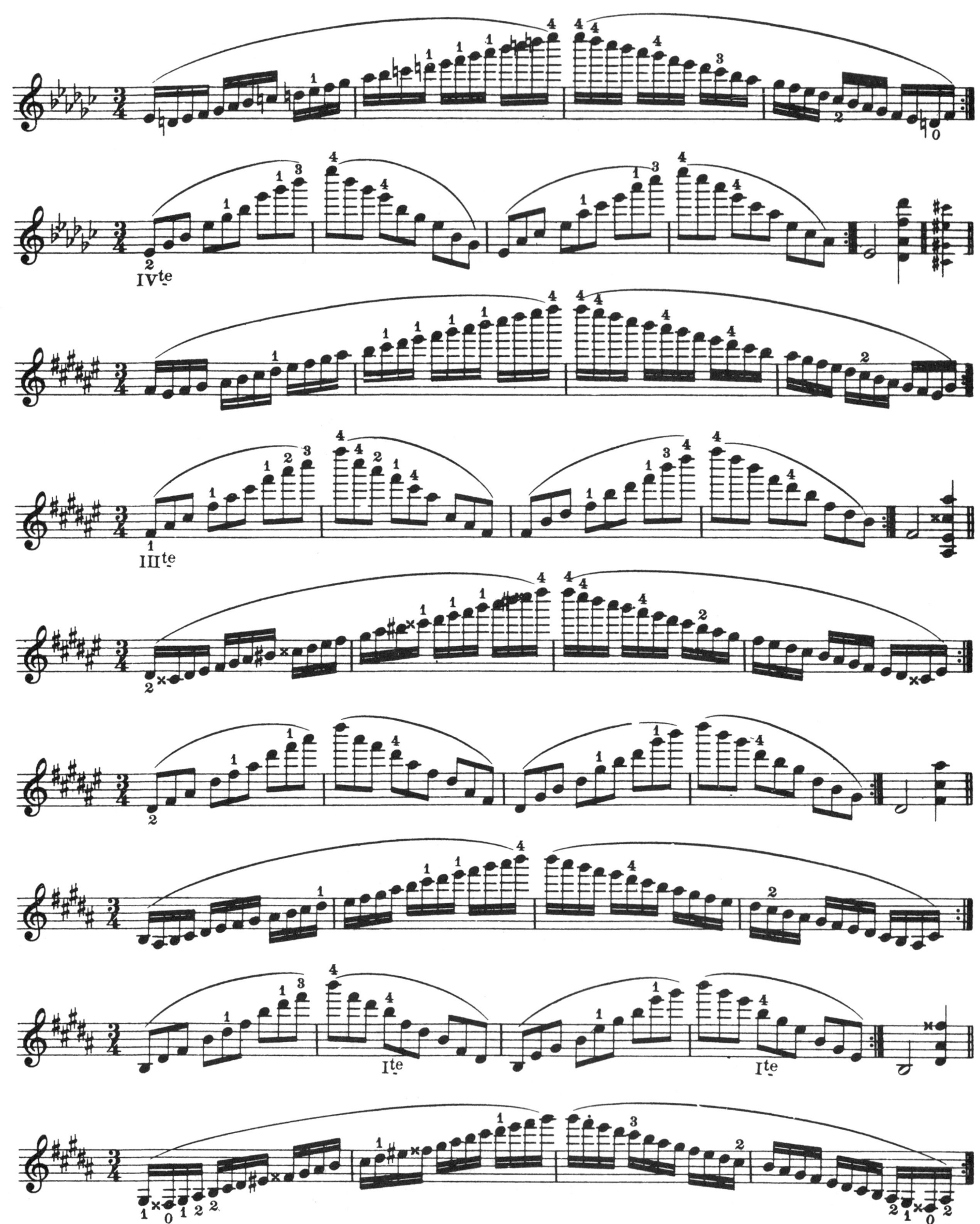

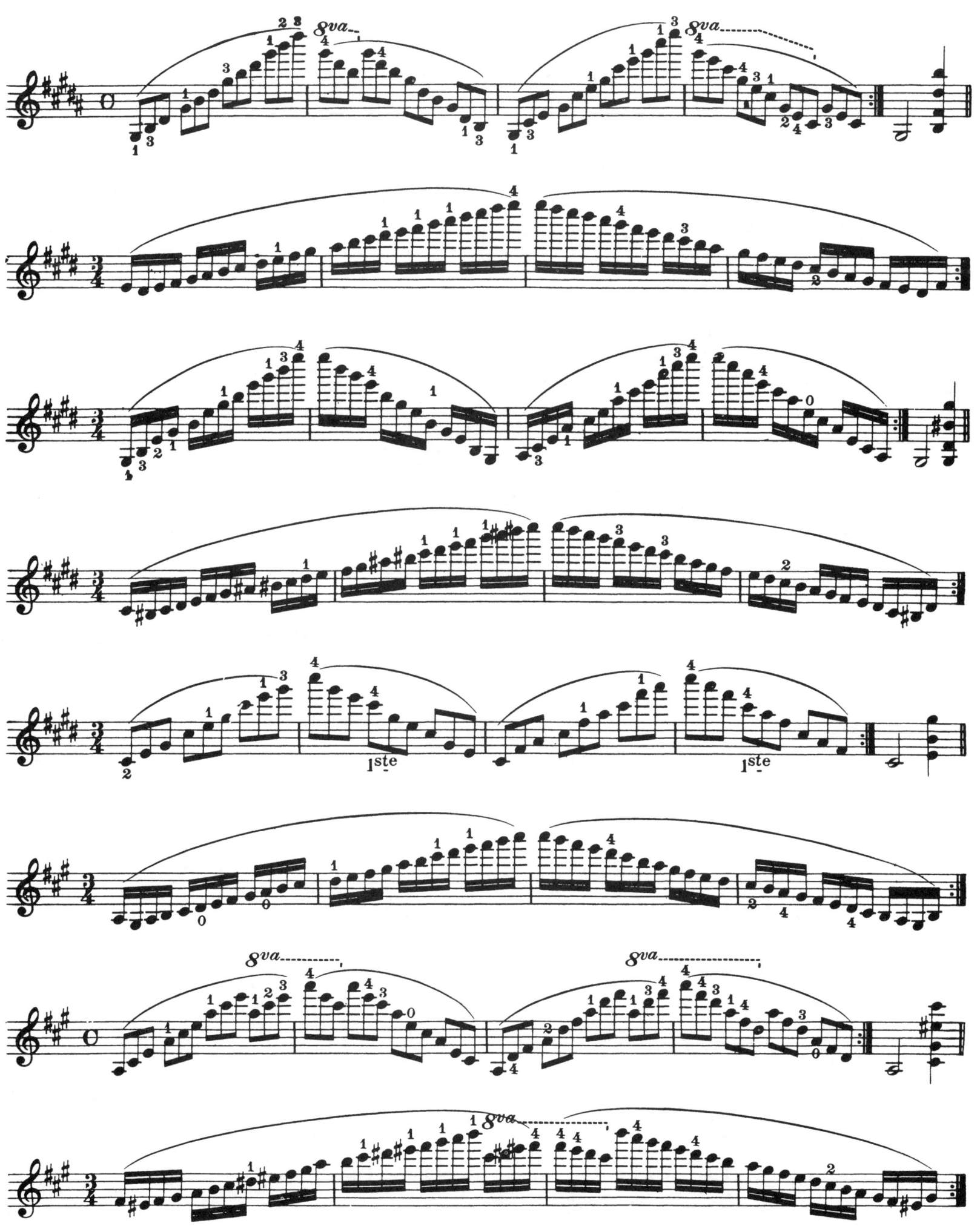

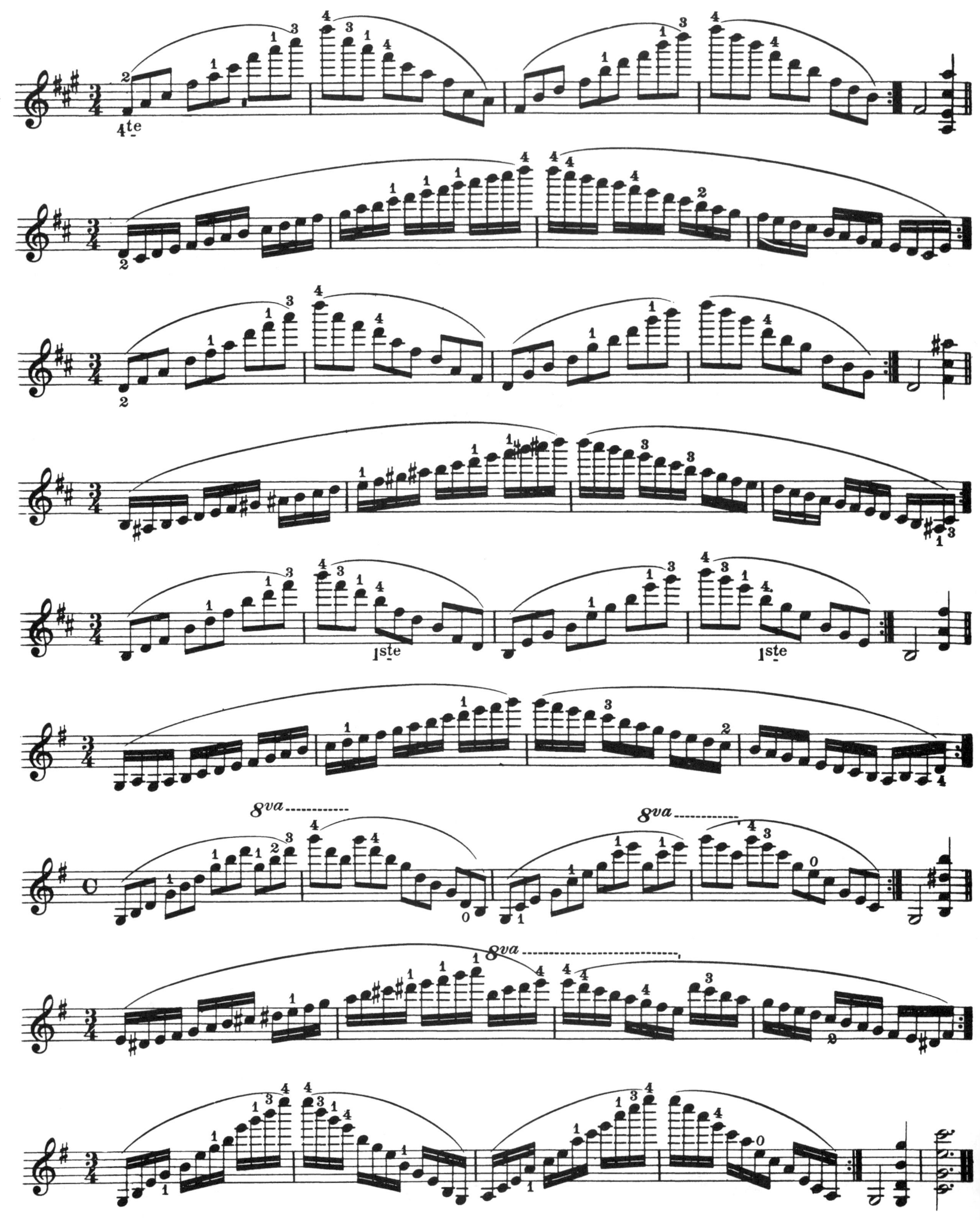

The Masters Collection

The Fritz Kreisler Collection
This collection features Kreisler's most popular original compositions, transcriptions and cadenzas for the violin in three volumes. Includes fabulous repertoire such as *Caprice Viennois, Liebesfreud, Liebeslied, Tango (Albeniz)* and the cadenzas for the Beethoven, Brahms and Paganini concertos. Compilations and introductory notes by Eric Wen. Forewords by Yehudi Menuhin and Isaac Stern.
Vol. 1 - ATF 115
Vol. 2 - ATF 124
Vol. 3 - ATF 125

The Heifetz Collection
Transcriptions & Cadenzas
This important collection contains 24 popular Heifetz transcriptions and two cadenzas for violin, including *Alt-Wien, Beau soir, Hora Staccato, Valse Bluette* and the cadenzas to Mozart's *Violin Concerto*, K. 218 and Brahms' *Violin Concerto*, Op. 77. Compilation and introductory notes by Eric Wen. Foreword by Itzhak Perlman.
ATF116

The Heifetz Collection, Vol. 2
Heifetz Plays Gershwin®
It is unfortunate that Gershwin never was able to write a violin concerto for Heifetz as promised. Heifetz incorporated the Gershwin sound into his repertoire through the performance of popular Gershwin themes such as *An American in Paris,* Five Selections from *Porgy and Bess,* and the *Three Preludes for Piano.**
ATF134

Includes never-before-published excerpts from *An American in Paris* ™

The Heifetz Collection, Vol. 3
Arrangements & Transcriptions
Newly discovered, never before published transcriptions and arrangements from violin master, Jascha Heifetz. Recently found by the Heifetz family, we proudly present the music of Zoltan Kodaly, Richard Strauss, Francis Poulenc, Sergei Prokofiev and many others meticulously and creatively arranged for violin and piano.
ATF142

* Gershwin, An American in Paris, and Porgy and Bess are all registered trademarks of Warner Bros. Music.

The Joseph Szigeti Collection
Transcriptions and Arrangements for Violin and Piano
Joseph Szigeti (1892–1973), was one of the outstanding violinists of the 20th century. A major inspiration for contemporary composers such as Bartók, Berg, Mihaud, Ravel and Stravinsky, Szigeti was known to perform and promote their repertoire. The transcriptions in this collection, compiled and edited by Eric Wen, contains some of his best work. Included in this collection: *Concerto in D Minor* (Tartini), *Passepied* from *Castor et Pollux* (Rameau), *Danse du Meunier* (Miller's Dance)from *The Three Cornered Hat* (de Falla) and four excerpts from *The Capriol Suite* by Peter Warlock.
ATF128

The Art of Violin Playing, Vol. 1
Carl Flesch, Edited by Eric Rosenblith
This new translation of Carl Flesch's *The Art of Violin Playing,* by Eric Rosenblith, preserves all of the basic concepts of Flesch's original, but presents them in more contemporary English. New hand diagrams have been added in addition to a table for the consistent use of bowing and fingering symbols. This essential book covers important topics such as: body posture, the left arm (positions & fingerings), vibrato, bowing (all varieties of strokes), tone production, musical memory and much more. This new edition of The Art of Violin Playing, Vol. 1 is one of today's most significant string publications.
O5365

Violin Methods by the Masters

LEOPOLD AUER

GRADED COURSE OF VIOLIN PLAYING

From the master teacher of the "masters,"—the most comprehensive and valuable method written. For the quick and dedicated, or older student. Also highly recommended for the advancing Suzuki player for introduction to note reading.

	Graded Course
O1416	Book 1—Preparatory
O1419	Book 2—Pre-Elementary
O1446	Book 3—Elementary
O1447	Book 4—Elementary, cont.
O1448	Book 5—Medium Advanced
O1449	Book 6—Advanced
O1450	Book 7—Difficult
O1451	Book 8—Virtuoso

MAIA BANG

VIOLIN METHOD

Based on the teaching principles of Leopold Auer. As sound and logical as when written, this time honored method is still "the" standard for beginning students. Utilizing Auer's principles Maia Bang's well-graded material provides ample exercises and songs at each level. This course of study leads the student to the development of solid technique and fine musicianship.

O42	Part 1—Elementary Rudiments (English ~ Spanish Texts)
O43	Part 2—More Advanced Studies
O44	Part 3—2nd ~ 3rd Positions
O45	Part 4—4th ~ 5th Positions
O46	Part 5—6th ~ 7th Positions
O47	Part 6—Higher Art of Bowing
O2498	Part 1—(English Text Only)

CARL FLESCH

O1317	THE ART OF VIOLIN PLAYING Book 1 — Technique in General and Applied Technique
O2046	Book 2 —Artistic Realization and Instruction
O205	BASIC STUDIES FOR VIOLIN
O2358	PROBLEMS OF TONE PRODUCTION IN VIOLIN PLAYING
O5188	SCALE SYSTEM Scale exercises in all major and minor keys

C.H. HOHMANN

PRACTICAL VIOLIN METHOD

O286	Book 1 —The open strings and preliminary exercises and pieces
O287	Book 2 — Exercises and pieces in the easiest keys
O288	Book 3 — Advanced exercises and pieces in all sharp and flat keys
O289	Book 4 — Exercises and pieces in the higher positions
O290	Book 5 — Exercises and pieces in the higher positions and of greater difficulty

GEORGE PERLMAN

O2779	THE VIOLINIST'S CONTEST ALBUM Fourteen compositions in the third position
	VIOLINISTS FIRST SOLO ALBUM
O2663	Vol. I-Elementary
O2664	Vol. 2-Intermediate
O4460	VIOLINIST'S RECITAL ALBUM A collection of stylistic solos